A Brief History of

COURIDJAH

In the Wollondilly Shire of New South Wales
Australia

Researched and transcribed by Karyn Chalk

A BRIEF HISTORY OF COURIDJAH IN THE WOLLONDILLY SHIRE OF NEW SOUTH WALES AUSTRALIA

ISBN: 978-1-4092-7612-8

Published by
Lulu.com

This book is dedicated to all the children of Couridjah, with special thanks to Adam, Alastair, Allan, Donata, Linda, Raewyn, Vanessa, Helen, Kate, Ron & everyone at the Picton & District Historical & Family History Society for all their contributions and support.

Introduction

This is a brief history of the town of Couridjah in the Wollondilly Shire of New South Wales, Australia.

This book outlines Couridjah's history, from its rich Aboriginal past through to its humble white beginnings when early settlers first arrived and established the village that we now know today as 'Couridjah'.

As well as supporting a wide range of endangered native wildlife, flora and fauna, Couridjah is host to some very significant historical and ecological sites such as the original Couridjah Train Station, Thirlmere Lakes and the old pump house building, the Tharawal Local Aboriginal Land Council and the existing Picton Lakes Village complex.

Couridjah Train Station, Apr 2007
Photograph taken & supplied by Alastair Chalk

Contents

Location

Couridjah is located approximately 90 kilometers south west of Sydney at the entry to the Southern Highlands of New South Wales. Within the Wollondilly Shire, it sits approximately 330 meters above sea level, supports a wide range of native wildlife, flora and fauna and is also host to some very significant historical and ecological sites.

Within Couridjah itself are situated the original Couridjah Train Station, the Thirlmere Lakes and old pump house building, the Tharawal Local Aboriginal Land Council plus the existing Picton Lakes Village complex and close by in Thirlmere is the Queen Victoria Memorial Hospital and Steam Train Museum. There are also plenty of fascinating places to be explored in the surrounding towns of Bargo, Buxton, Picton, Tahmoor and Thirlmere.

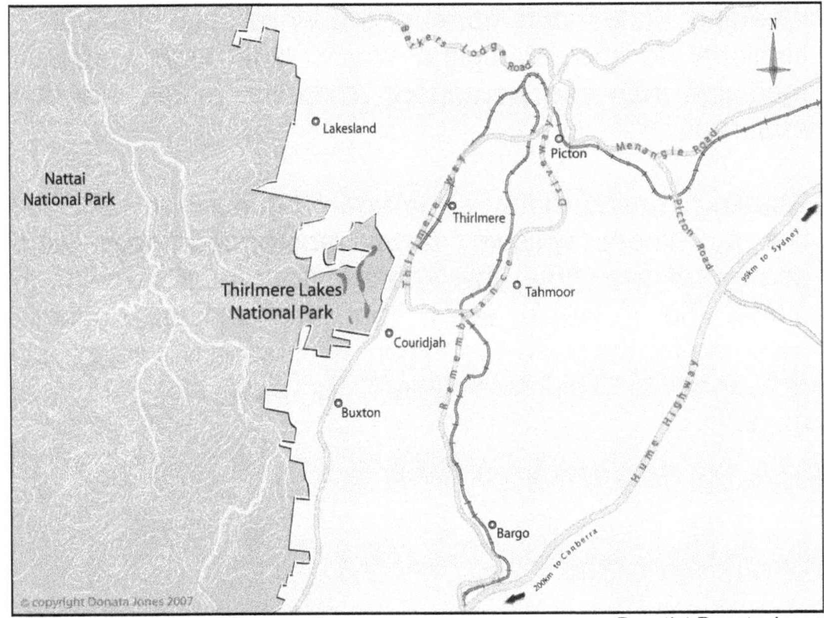

Map of Couridjah and Surrounds By artist Donata Jones

The origin of the word 'Couridjah'

The word Couridjah originates from an Aboriginal word and has many documented translations but these often tend to represent the apparent observations of white man at the time. For example, explorer George Caley, who was incidentally a botanist, recorded Couridjah to mean 'the place where banksia trees grow'. It had been noted that the local Aboriginal people referred to the lakes as a place of 'coradgery' which was mistaken for the lakes having been called 'Coradgery' however it is also documented that the local Aboriginal name for the lakes was actually a word sounding like 'Nerrigorang', apparently meaning 'water with a sandy bottom'. Couridjah has also been translated as meaning 'honey' and 'home of the white ants' although it's similarity to the Aboriginal words 'kooradgie', meaning medicine man and 'coradgery', meaning magic, are quite apparent.

Keeping in mind that spelling and pronunciation will, much like a Chinese whisper, have transformed these words somewhat over time, the 'kooradj' sound still remains the same. So it would seem that the original Aboriginal meaning for the word 'Couridjah' was actually, with specific reference to Thirlmere Lakes, *'a place for Aboriginal magic'.*

Aboriginal Inhabitants

The Aboriginal inhabitants who roamed the Couridjah area were known as the 'Gundungurra' or 'Gundagurra' tribe. Their chief in 1802, as documented by explorer, Barrallier, was named 'Goondel'. He was apparently succeeded by 'Young Bundle' and the last recorded chief was 'Murrengurry', who died in 1857 and was buried 2½ miles from Argyle St, Picton. Local Aboriginals were referred to by settlers as the 'cowpasture tribe' due to a herd of wild cattle being found (after 6 head had escaped from the Sydney settlement previously) living there in 1795. The medicine men in the tribe were called 'kooradgies' and they were said to have made magic using crystals which they carried around their necks in a leather pouch. Although the medicine men were renowned for their powers of healing and vision, it was also said that a kooradgie could cause death to a man by simply pointing a bone in their direction so their power was apparently not something to be reckoned with. These men were said to have been chosen on their superior intelligence and insight and were very highly regarded within the tribe.

According to Bill Hardie, Chairman of the Gundungurra Tribal Council, the homelands of the Gundungurra included the lands and waters of Burragorang, Megalong, Kanimbla, Jamison and Hartley Valleys to Lithgow, Clarence and Wallerawang; west over to the watershed ridge above the O'Connell Plains and the water-Catchment of the Abercrombie River; east of the Lachlan River, to south of Goulburn and Bungonia including the Wombeyan and Jenolan Caves and east to Bundanoon, Bowral, Picton, Warragamba, Penrith and Springwood to Katoomba. Gundungurra people not only lived within a territorial area but they also spoke the Gundungurra language. Although there appear to be no fluent Gundungurra speakers alive today, many descendants know individual words. Using published accounts and unpublished manuscripts, James Kohen, author of 'The Darug and Their Neighbours – The traditional Aboriginal owners of the Sydney region', has compiled two lists of over five hundred words and phrases spoken by the Gundungurra and asserts that it was bounded in the west by the Wiradjuri language, on the north and east by the Dharug (Darug) language, and in the south by the Ngunawal language. The Dharouk tribe was located on their northern boundary, the Thurrawal tribe lived between the Nepean river and the coast and on the south eastern side were situated the Wodi-Wodi tribe. To the west were the Wiradjuri tribesmen.

Exact numbers of Aboriginal people in the area before colonization were not recorded however Kohen states that corroborees were witnessed in the Camden area up until as late as the 1820's with approximately 400 local and visiting Aboriginals having been sighted in attendance at any one time. They held initiation ceremonies annually where different tribes met and also had special meeting places along the rivers, like on the banks of Myrtle creek, where they would exchange gemstones such as crystals from the Wollondilly area (Which were very popular amongst the Aboriginals due to their being used by the highly respected kooradgies.) for black basalt (Used for axe making.) from the Kiama district. They also traded in roots and honey and exchanged girls between tribes for marriage.

The number of members of the Gundungurra tribe was not ever recorded to be in excess of 200 at any one time and their numbers rapidly dwindled away during the 1800s due to their lack of immunity to newly introduced European diseases along with the white settler's occupation of former Aboriginal hunting and food bearing land. White man's refusal to share this land with its original Aboriginal inhabitants was inconceivable to the Aboriginal people. It seriously impeded their means of survival and entire way of life, which had proven successful to Aboriginal Australians thriving across the continent for the past 40,000+ years.

Altercations arose around this predicament which resulted in combat. The government endorsed harsh Aboriginal persecutions which culminated in an horrific massacre of local Aboriginal people at Cataract Gorge, Appin on the 17th April 1816. The few remaining Gundungurra people moved out to the area around The Oaks until about the year 1900, when no pure blooded natives were left locally.

In the 1920s the remnant of the tribe moved to a reserve in La Perouse where they were forced to live, work and made to surrender their children, as per Government policy (or have them forcibly removed) in a barbaric practice which then forbade Aboriginal children to practice ceremonies or even speak their language and only ceased in the 1960s.

'Circle of Life' By Aboriginal artist Linda Williams

Early Settlers

The first European exploration of the area surrounding Picton was conducted by a party led by ex-convict John Wilson in 1798 however surveys for settlement in the area were not carried out until 1821. Being part of the Cowpastures, it had been up until that time, proclaimed out of bounds to protect the wild cattle who were descendants of the two bulls and four cows which had escaped from the infant colony in Sydney back in 1788.

A few early settlers took up blocks around the lagoons in the early 1820s but as the roads to that area were not yet properly established, early village life must have been very rustic and isolated. By the mid 1830s, settlers had established themselves on the better soil towards Cedar Creek and parts of Lakesland had also been taken up. They grew hay, corn and vegetables and kept bees, cows and poultry. By the 1840's the area supported a large number of firewood cutters who would take their loads by bullock wagons or horse teams bound for Sydney.

From the 1860's settlement expanded with land being acquired through conditional purchase. In mid 1884, a minor land boom set in then in 1913 subdivisions opened up smaller parcels of land to new settlers. By the mid 1920's, growth had slowed and the area was being surveyed by the government as a site for the future Picton Lakes consumptives village. The population increased significantly in the post-war years, spurred by the opening of coal mines in the 1960s and 1970s and has continued to attract both local workers and commuters from Sydney, showing a steady stream of growth into the new century.

Residence of man in charge at Picton Lakes Pumping Station, Oct 1884
Photograph taken by H.A. Lenehan & supplied by PDH&FHS

Ex residence of man in charge at Picton Lakes Pumping Station, Aug 2007
Photograph taken and supplied by Alastair Chalk

Thirlmere Lakes

Thirlmere Lakes is a small system of five perennial freshwater lakes within the Thirlmere Lakes National Park, a 627 hectare area which became a national park in 1974. The lake system is estimated to have been formed approximately 15 million years ago by rare geomorphologic processes and contains at least 30 meters of sandy alluvium. Initial formation had been suggested around a Middle Miocene age, however, more recent mapping assigns a Late Cretaceous to Early Tertiary age. In any instance, its survival until today is extraordinarily unique.

This level of remarkable stability has allowed the evolution of a number of rare species in isolation, including the freshwater sponge, *Radiospongilla sceptroides*, and the water lily, *Brasenia schreberi.* Accordingly, the aquatic habitats within Thirlmere Lakes National Park support many organisms which are restricted or almost restricted to this one lake system. There are a number of planktonic and bottom-dwelling protozoans (single celled animals or colonies of single celled animals) present, both along the shores and in the limnetic zone (the top layer of open lake waters which is penetrated by light). Crustaceans are an important part of the bottom-dwelling fauna and are an integral part of the lake ecology. The Greater Blue Mountains Area (Including Thirlmere Lakes National Park.) is famous for containing many ancient, relict species of great global significance.

The first white men to discover the lakes were members of the party led by John Wilson in March of 1798. Then in November of the year 1802, explorer Francis Barrallier again came across what is today known as the Thirlmere Lakes. Although the Lakes original Aboriginal name was actually a word sounding like 'Nerrigorang' it was assumed by early surveyors to have been a word sounding like 'Couridjah', so hence was the name later given to the station on the railway line nearby, growing in time to encompass the surrounding township of Couridjah. The Aboriginal inhabitants of the lakes area apparently spoke of the lakes as a place of 'coradgery' which lent its name to the lakes initially as the 'Coradgery Lagoons'. They were briefly known as 'Picton Lakes' around the early 1900's and had also been referred to as Bargo or Picton Lagoons. During the operation of the Great Southern Railway loop line, the lakes served as the main water source for the Picton / Mittagong sector. Water was pumped from the third lake, via a pumphouse up to Couridjah train station where the steam trains would stop to fill their tanks.

The lakes remain as magical as ever and now serve as a popular tourist destination. Perfect for picnics, swimming, bushwalking and photography, Thirlmere lakes are open to the public daily, from sunrise to sunset.

Thirlmere Lakes, May 2007
Photograph taken & supplied by Vanessa Giannikouris

Picton Lakes, (Now known as Thirlmere Lakes) Oct 1884
Photograph taken by H.A. Lenehan & supplied by PDH&FHS

Thirlmere Lakes, (Formerly known as Picton Lakes) May 2007
Photograph taken & supplied by Vanessa Giannikouris

The old pump house at Thirlmere Lakes, May 2007
Photograph taken & supplied by Vanessa Giannikouris

Picton Lakes Pumping Station, Oct 1884
Photograph taken by H.A. Lenehan & supplied by PDH&FHS

Couridjah Train Station

Couridjah Train Station, May 2007
Photograph taken & supplied by Vanessa Giannikouris

From 1863-67 the Great Southern Railway Line was under construction between Picton and Mittagong. The train line was officially opened on the 1st March 1867. A pumping station was established at Picton Lakes and a stone cottage was built up near the railway line. The station was initially opened at the commencement of the line as a 'water tank only', under the name of 'Picton Lagoons Tank'. The passenger platform was then built and officially opened on the 6th September 1869 but the name 'Picton Lakes' didn't actually appear in the timetable until 21st April 1879. This station was later named 'Couridjah' and serviced the Tahmoor/Bargo area. The line remained in use as the major route between Picton and Mittagong until the deviation opened in 1919. In 1954, all sidings were removed from Couridjah station, leaving only the platform and shed remaining when regular use of the old loop line ceased. It has since been maintained and used as an historical steam train route and has also featured in various television shows and commercials.

The old loop line was described in this account of the train journey made by Francis Meyers, F. J. Broomfield and J. P. Dowling in 1886:

'At Picton the railway begins the ascent to the tableland, the gradient on leaving the station being one in thirty-three; within a distance of six miles there is a rise of over five hundred feet, at which point the engines stay their course to replenish their tanks. This is done from a chain of lagoons on the right known as the Picton Lakes, lying in the broadened bed of a sandstone gully —a rough and uninviting country, densely timbered, and but little used. A few miles to the east is the darkly-famed Bargo Brush —a primitive forest, through which ran the southern road, and which, in days of old, gave shelter and concealment to many bold and bloodthirsty bushrangers, whose dark and sanguinary deeds have inscribed the name of Bargo on the crimson calendar of crime, for in outlaw lore it stands even before Eugowra and Glenrowan.'

Steam train leaving Picton Lakes, Couridjah, Oct 1884
Photograph taken by H.A. Lenehan & supplied by PDH&FHS

Steam train arriving Couridjah, May 2007
Photograph taken and supplied by Alastair Chalk

Picton Lakes Village

The original village land grant of 124 acres was situated at Couridjah on the east side of the train line on what is now known as East Parade. The current site still remains on a portion of the original grant. It was established as a self contained consumptive village for soldiers and sailors with tuberculosis. The location was selected for it's isolation from the public along with the fresh air and high elevation having been promoted as being healthier for patients who were suffering from tuberculosis. Having been designed by architect George H.Goodsell, the village was opened on the 16th June 1927 by Sir J.Joynton Smith, the then President of the Picton Lakes Village Settlement along with Admiral Sir Dudley De Chair , who was the Governor of New South Wales at that time.

Official party at Picton Lakes TB Settlement Site, Couridjah - 1927
Photograph supplied by PDH&FHS

Tuberculosis treatment and patient isolation management was causing grave concerns amongst Sydneysiders during the mass TB outbreak of the 1920s. The convalescent settlement concept was introduced to promote a healing environment for TB patients in a remote location in order to minimise patient distress and contain the spread of infection. The Picton Lakes Village served as a TB settlement until the disease was no longer a national health issue.

Picton Lakes Village remains in near original condition and currently serves as staff accommodation, running under ownership of the Queen Victoria Memorial Hospital.

Picton Lakes Village, May 2007
Photograph taken & supplied by Vanessa Giannikouris

Queen Victoria Memorial Hospital

The Queen Victoria Hospital comprises of a large complex of buildings established by Colonel John Hay Goodlet, a wealthy merchant who purchased the land and originally built the hospital as a home for consumptives after the sad loss of his sister to tuberculosis. Goodlet House was built in 1886 and operated until Queen Victoria Homes for Consumptives took it over in 1897. It was converted to an aged care facility in the nineteen fifties and continues to function as one today.

The Polyclinic, Nursing Administration and Administration buildings are brick structures dating from 1907. The Repatriation Chalet was built in 1947, specifically for ex-servicewomen who had contracted tuberculosis when serving in the war. The grounds include the main driveway avenue, courtyard gardens and an original tree planting near the Chalets. There are dams and early fence lines still in place from the previous rural use of the property.

Queen Victoria Memorial Hospital, May 2007
Photograph taken & supplied by Vanessa Giannikouris

Early Local Influential Personalities

BARALLIER, Francis (1773-1853)

Francis Barallier arrived in Australia in April 1800. He was appointed an ensign in the New South Wales Corps in July 1800 and was made engineer and artillery officer in August 1801. He was directed by Governor Philip Gidley King in November 1802 to try to find a way over the Blue Mountains to the west of Sydney. Although he did not succeed in crossing the range, he was one of the earliest explorers to document the local area. His finishing point was "*towards the head of Christy's Creek, about 15 or 16 miles in a direct line southerly from Jenolan Caves.*"

CALEY, George (1770-1829)

As a botanist sent to survey the 'New World', Caley arrived in Australia in 1800. Sir Joseph Banks had asked for permission to send Caley to New South Wales in 1798. Caley assessed the local area and also undertook many successful collecting trips to the north, south and west of Sydney however his journey into the Blue Mountains was his most challenging and impacted the rest of his life.

DE CHAIR, Admiral Sir Dudley (1864 – 1958)

De Chair became governor of New South Wales in October 1923, arriving in Sydney with his wife on 28 February 1924. He quickly formed a close friendship with Nationalist premier Sir George Fuller and was part responsible for the opening of the Picton Lakes Village Settlement.

FOWLER, Lillian (1887-1954)

Lillian Fowler was the director of Picton Lakes TB Settlement in Couridjah and an executive member of the

Women's Voluntary National Register from 1939 until 1940. She became the first woman Alderman in NSW in 1929 and the first woman Mayor in Australia in1938-39.

JONES, Sir Philip Sydney (1836-1918)
A physician and surgeon, born on 15 April 1836 in Sydney, Jones strongly believed in the open-air treatment of tuberculosis and was a founder of the Queen Victoria Homes for Consumptives which in 1897 took over J. H. Goodlet's sanatorium at Thirlmere. He published several papers on the dissemination and treatment of tuberculosis and 1905 he was knighted for his work in combating the disease.

JOYNTON SMITH, Sir James John (1858-1943)
Sir James John Joynton Smith first came to Sydney in about 1890. He was first president of the Picton Lakes T.B. Soldiers and Sailors' Settlement. His autobiography, '*My Life Story*' (1927), ghosted by Claude McKay, showed his relish for business intrigue and speculative investments; 'to succeed in business one should always be in debt', he wrote. He backed innovative ventures such as Sydney's first radio station 2SB (2BL).

MARSHALL, Andrew (1897-1960)
In October of 1929, Marshall married Agnes (Nancy) Hood Fenwick. Moving his practice to Picton that year, he became visiting medical officer at the Queen Victoria Sanatorium, Thirlmere, and at the Picton Lakes Village, Couridjah, thereby beginning his lifelong involvement in the treatment of tuberculosis. In 1939 he sold his Picton practice. Andrew's interests included photography and contract bridge, but his greatest passion was for golf: he was a champion club player and a dedicated member of

the Picton, Leura and Killara clubs. He was also a director of the Queen Victoria Homes for Consumptives.

PICKARD, Charles Henry (1800s – 1900s)

Charles Henry Pickard was the leading citizen of the locality from 1885 -1920. He owned several shops in the district with the main one being at Thirlmere. His other stores were situated at Bargo, Bowral, Colo Vale, Kangaloon, Mittagong, Picton and The Oaks. They were all connected with a private telephone line before the post offices at Camden and Picton had the phone line connected. In 1919 his health grew frail and hence he was succeeded as general manager by his son, Henry Jasper Pickard. C.H Pickard introduced the Jerusalem Artichoke to Australia and also returned from a trip to England bearing a new fodder crop called Helianti.

C.H. Pickard's store, Oaks Road, Thirlmere – opened in 1887
Photograph supplied by PDH&FHS

RACKLYEFT, George John (1879-1952)

G.J. Racklyeft, an early owner of an acreage with direct lake access, along with W.E. Middleton and J. Slade made efforts to have a wider road cut through to allow public access down to Thirlmere Lakes in the late 1930's however it was not until the 1950's that the family cleared a large area of the lakes shores, sewed grass, planted shrubs and trees and then again approached council to widen the road when permission was finally granted.

WILSON, John (– 1800)
A convict who was sentenced to transportation from England for having stolen nine yards of cotton cloth in October of 1785, at Wigan, Lancashire. Wilson arrived in Sydney aboard the First Fleet in January 1788. After the expiration of his seven year term, he retreated to the bush and spent several years living amongst the Aboriginals, to whom he was known as 'Bun-bo-e'. During this time he attended ceremonies, dressed in native attire and acquired an extensive knowledge of the surrounding countryside. Having finally returned to the settlement by 1797, Wilson was recruited to guide a party of explorers into what was then referred to as the 'New World' which was about 200 miles south-west of Sydney. During his first expedition in 1798 and then another made shortly afterwards, he reached as far as Goulburn. Wilson was accompanied by two other men on each occasion, (One of whom, being 19 year old John Price, recorded his observations which are now held at the Mitchell Library.) Wilson was noted to have been responsible for their ultimate survival. By 1799, John Wilson had reverted back to his life in the wild however in 1800 was killed by an Aboriginal for breaking tribal law by attempting to abduct a young woman from the tribe for his own gratuitous pleasures.

YAGER, Arthur William (1884 - 1967)
Born in Redfern, NSW, Yager married Jane Gabriel on the 29th of November, 1913 and they had 2 sons. He was secretary and chief executive at Picton Lakes TB Village Settlement 1947-1968.

References

Flood, Josephine: 'The Riches of Ancient Australia – A Journey into Prehistory' published Australia, 1990
Flood, Josephine: 'Rock Art of the Dreamtime' Published Australia, 1997
Isaacs, Jennifer: 'Australian Dreaming 40,000 Years of Aboriginal History' published Australia, 1980
Kohen, James: 'The Darug and their neighbours – The traditional Aboriginal Owners of Australia' published Australia, 1993
Mulvaney, John and Kamminga, John: 'Prehistory of Australia' published Australia, 1999
Tweedie, Penny: 'Aboriginal Australians Spirit of Arnhem Land' published Australia, 1998

http://www.adb.online.anu.edu.au
http://www.anbg.gov.au
http://www.anzacatt.org.au
http://www.aussieheritage.com.au
http://www.eniar.org
http://www.geocities.com
http://www.gundungurra.net.au
http://www.gutenberg.net.au
http://www.parliament.nsw.gov.au
http://www.stonequarry.com.au
http://www.nationalparks.nsw.gov.au
http://www.phansw.org.au
http://www.regional.org.au
http://www.smh.com.au
http://www.takver.com
http://www.users.acenet.com.au
http://www.whereis.com
http://www.wollemipine.com
http://www.wollondilly.nsw.gov.au

With special thanks for:

Aboriginal art 'Circle of Life' by Linda Karen Williams

Cover & local photography by Vanessa Giannikouris

Local photography by Alastair Chalk

Map of Couridjah and surrounds by Donata Jones

Also with special thanks to the Picton and District Historical and Family History Society for the provision of all previously referenced historical photographs plus:

Chalker, Stephen – 'C.H.Pickard' in The Stonequarry Journal Vol 6, No 3, Sep 1992
History of The Thirlmere Lakes by W.Rackleyft, April 1962
Knox, F.B. 'A Brief Sketch', March 1975
Singleton, C.C. - 'Centenary of the opening of the Southern Line to Mittagong' in the Australian Railway Historical Society Bulletin No.353, March 1967

www.ingramcontent.com/pod-product-compliance
Ingram Content Group UK Ltd.
Pitfield, Milton Keynes, MK11 3LW, UK
UKHW020227250726
13967UKWH00001B/227